LEARN TO DRAW 3-D

by DOUG DuBOSQUE

SCHOLASTIC INC.

New York Toronto London Auckland Sydney

Special thanks to pre-publication reviewers:
- Jan Lamont and the students of Maplewood School, Edmonds, Washington;
- Charlotte Seymour and the students of Bridlemile School, Portland, Oregon;
- Rita Whitt, Sandy Blondino, and the students of Bonney Lake School in Sumner, Washington!

And to:
- Pat Brigandi, who gave valuable ideas after reviewing *Learn To Draw NOW!*
- My patient editor and wife, Susan Joyce DuBosque…

…all of whom helped me keep this project in perspective.

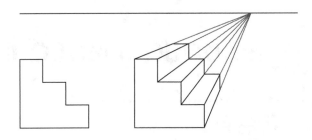

ISBN 0-590-03740-4

12 11 10 9 8 7 6 5   8 9/9 0 1 2 3/0

Printed in the U.S.A.   40

First Scholastic printing, September 1998

LEARN TO DRAW 3-D

CONTENTS

ABOUT THIS BOOK

This book shows how to create depth in drawings, so that viewers think they're looking into the distance. 3-D means "three-dimensional." When you draw lines on a paper, they go up and down, side to side, diagonally, or in curves, but they always lie flat on the paper. The paper really has just two dimensions, height and width. In other words, up and down, or side to side. There isn't any third dimension on flat paper.

To make something look far away, you have to organize the marks you use—whether lines, dots, or carefully blended colors—so that the person looking at your picture feels that parts of it are closer, and parts of it are farther away. That's where 3-D comes into the picture—as an illusion that you create. You've noticed that objects look smaller farther away. Also, colors seem less bright, or less intense, in the distance. When you bring those observations to your drawing, you create the feeling of depth.

Perhaps you've also looked at the lines of a road, sidewalks, railroad tracks, and power lines as they run into the distance. In your drawings, you can use these lines to create a feeling of depth. In the pages that follow, we'll explore the use of lines to create depth in pictures. You'll make some fun discoveries, so let's get started!

What you need:

1) Pencil—longer than your finger, please;
2) Pencil sharpener—somewhere nearby;
3) Eraser—bigger than the one on your pencil!;
4) Ruler (or straightedge; we won't measure much);
5) Paper—I use "junk" paper to practice—backs of old photocopies and computer printouts.

Attention teachers!

I've done my best to take a complicated, fascinating subject and break it into bite-sized hunks. I've tried to make each section something that can be used in a classroom by a teacher who isn't an art specialist, but who is willing to try something new. I've also tried to keep lessons open-ended, to encourage students to make imaginative use of their newly-acquired skills. My goal is a compelling and success-oriented introduction, but perhaps I've skipped something, or perhaps I haven't gone far enough. I'd enjoy hearing your suggestions (or just reactions) for 'fine-tuning' future editions—and also ideas for other *Learn To Draw* books!   —D.D.

CHAPTER 1
THE STARTING POINT

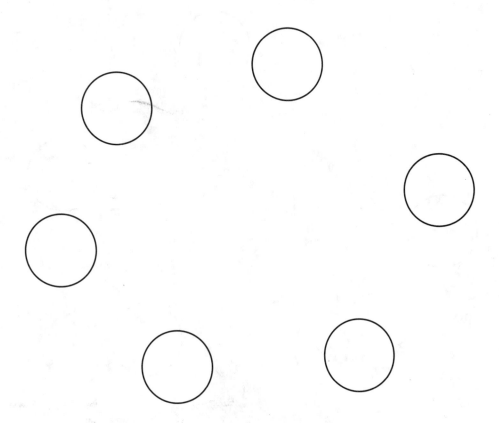

We'll start out simply. Grab a sheet of paper and a pencil, and something with a straight edge—like a ruler. On the paper, draw a few circles, or ovals—nothing more.

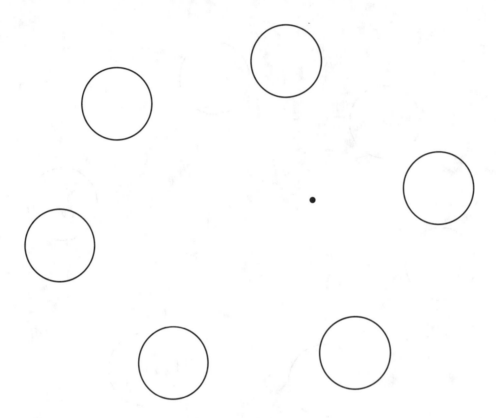

Now make a dot somewhere in the middle of the ovals. My dot is bigger than it needs to be. Yours can be tiny; make it just big enough, and just dark enough, that you can see it. (You'll be using that dot many times—it's called the *vanishing point*.)

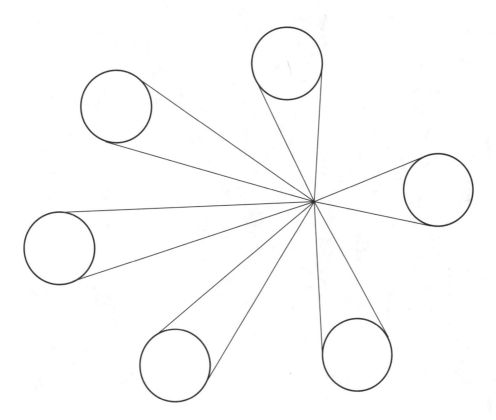

Next take your ruler, and make straight lines from the center dot to the outside edges of the ovals, or circles. Feel free to turn your paper sideways or upside down while drawing the lines.

When you're done, take a look at your drawing. Does it look like something going far away from you, or rushing towards you? That's the whole point (at least the whole point of the vanishing point).

You don't have to stick with simple shapes—you can make your drawing more complicated if you wish. Some lines disappear behind the shape. In this drawing, lines disappear behind part of the stars.

Of course, when you make things more complicated, it's easier to make mistakes. I made this picture more complicated. And I made a mistake. Look carefully. Can you see anything I left out?

Line from the top point of one of the stars...

You can have fun experimenting with this type of one-point perspective. And don't just stick to black and white—experiment with colors. Generally, bolder, brighter colors will appear to be closer to you—duller colors will appear farther away. Also, warmer colors—orange, red-orange, yellow-orange—will appear to be closer to you, while blues and blue-greens may appear to be farther away.

Here's a way to use one-point perspective if you want to make a poster, or decorate something with words. Once again, remember what happens as you make your drawing more complicated—you're more likely to make mistakes. As in my earlier drawing, it happens I forgot something in this one. Can you spot it?

First letter 'E' in 'HERE'...

CHAPTER 2
ONE-POINT PERSPECTIVE

Vanishing Point

•

Let's return to our single dot, the vanishing point. Draw a line for the horizon, and put a dot for the vanishing point somewhere towards the center of it. The *horizon* is *horizontal* —think about it. The horizon represents your eye level, as far as you can see. There might be mountains above the horizon, or scenery blocking the horizon, but the horizon is always there—your eye level, as far as you can see. The horizon becomes a very important part of your drawing, so draw it carefully. Use a ruler if you want to.

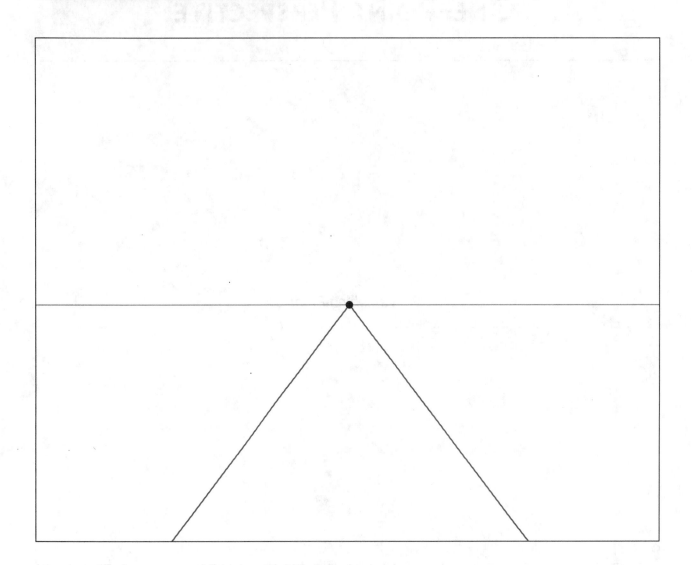

From the vanishing point, draw two straight lines to the bottom of the page. Does it look like a pyramid in the middle of the desert? It could be, if you stopped here, but…

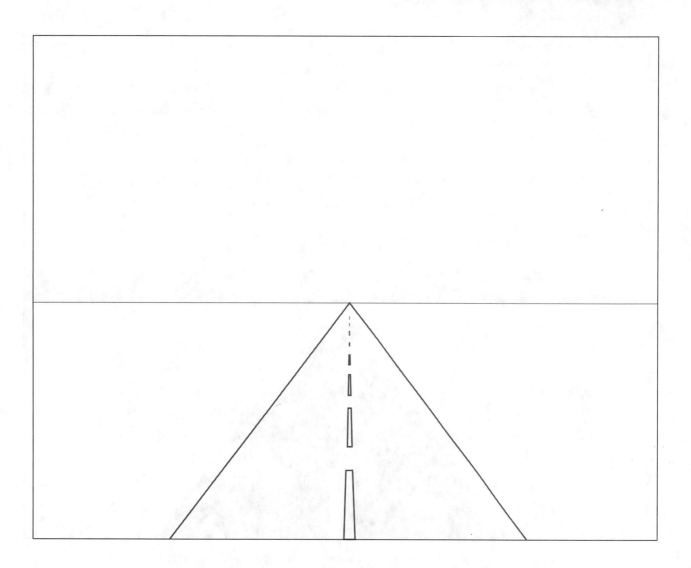

…when you add a broken line down the middle, it turns into a road, running far into the distance—all the way to the horizon. Notice how the pieces of the line get smaller as they appear farther away. In this drawing, "farther away" means closer to the vanishing point.

Take a moment, and look at your drawing—does this road remind you of a video game? It should—compare this with the road in a video game (one small difference—the road in the video game may not extend all the way to the vanishing point).

▼ **IMPORTANT!**
From now on, draw lines very lightly at first, so you can erase them later. Some won't be part of the finished picture!

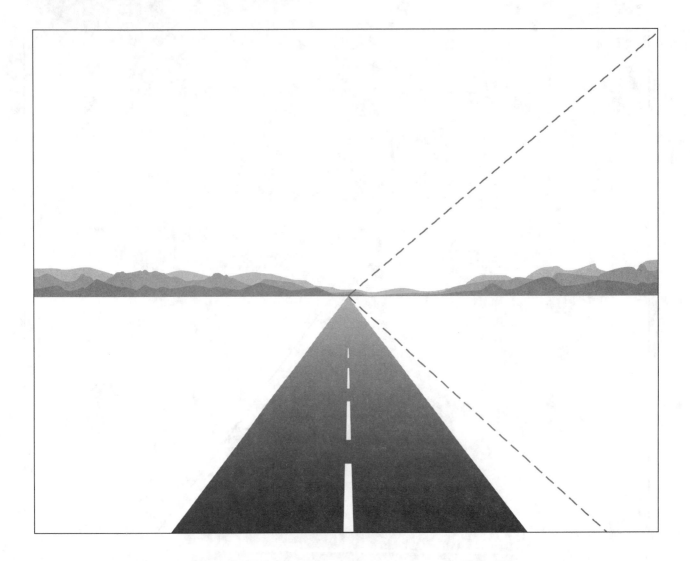

Next, let's add some mountains. In this one-point perspective drawing, objects farther away (closer to the horizon) usually look smaller. They also appear more gray. Keep this in mind as you draw: there is less contrast in objects far away. If the road is black and white right in front of you, at a greater distance it will be dark gray and light gray. The same is true for the mountains.

Next add two more light guide lines, one below the horizon and one above the horizon. It doesn't matter if they run off the top, side, or bottom of the page—just make sure they start from the vanishing point. And make sure they're straight!

Next we're going to add a power pole. Remember this:

1) The power poles all go straight up and down. They don't lean!
   (Lay your pencil vertically on the paper—going up and down
   exactly like the side of the page. That's the way the pole goes—
   straight up and down.)
2) The top of each power pole meets the top guide line, and the
   bottom of each power pole meets the bottom guideline—they stop
   at the guide lines, and run right through the horizon. (Notice that
   the pole blocks off the horizon—you can't see anything through the
   solid pole.)

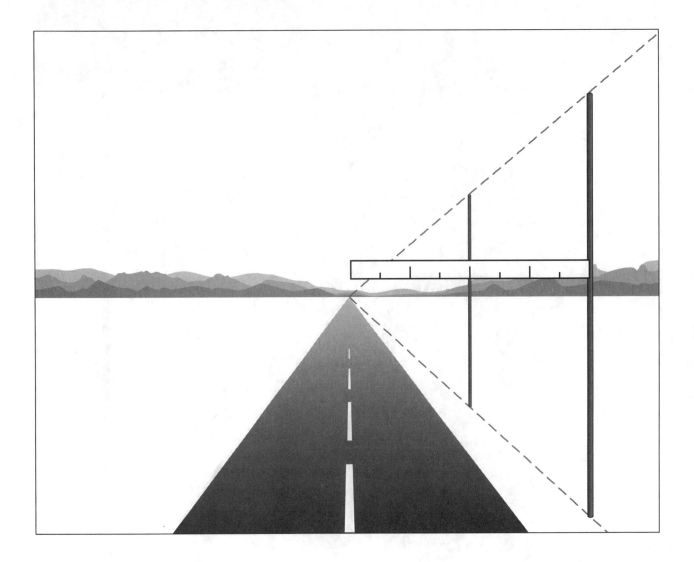

Once you have one power pole in place, look at the horizon again and find a point on it halfway between the first power pole and the vanishing point. Now draw the second pole halfway between the first power pole and the vanishing point. Like the first pole, the second pole runs straight up and down from the top guide line to the bottom guide line.

When you have two poles drawn, you can add a third pole, halfway between the second pole and the vanishing point. Like the other poles, make it run straight up and down from the top guide line to the bottom guide line. Check again to make sure it doesn't lean!

And so it goes, with smaller and smaller power poles all the way to the vanishing point. Each pole runs straight up and down! (If your poles lean, remember to look at the edge of the paper, which runs straight up and down—your poles should be *parallel* to the edge of the paper.)

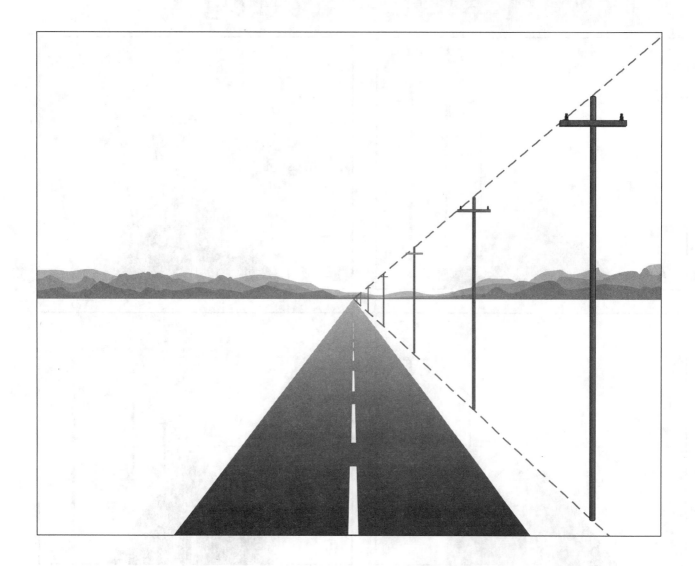

To hold the wires on the power poles, add cross arms. The cross arms are horizontal, just like the horizon. Look at how they get smaller and smaller, just as the power poles get smaller and smaller.

TIME OUT!

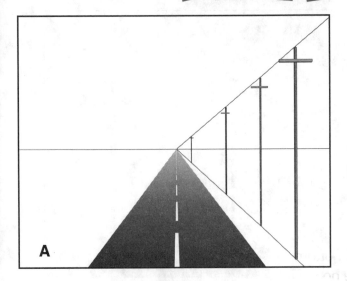

A

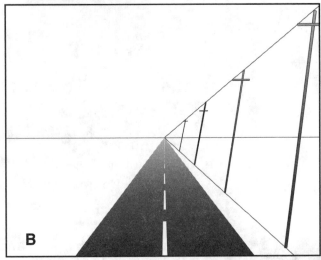

B

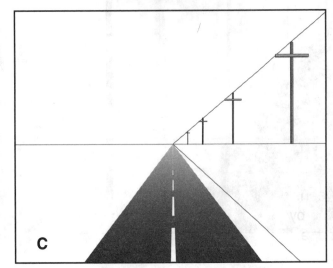

C

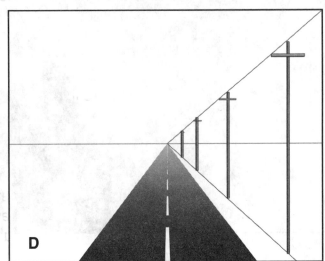

D

Let's pause for a moment. Here are four common errors—what's wrong with each picture? Check your drawing to make sure you haven't made the same errors. If you have, correct them, or just start over—it will be quicker the second time. (Honest!)

Answers—A: Distance between poles doesn't get smaller closer to the vanishing point. B: Poles lean! C: Instead of running between guide lines, poles stop at the horizon. D: Poles are the same thickness— more distant poles should be thinner.

TIME OUT!

<<< What's wrong here?

Remember, the cross arms need to be horizontal. They don't follow the diagonal guide line to the vanishing point. They go from *side to side* on your page.

Something else you might not be too sure about is what the tops and bottoms of the poles should look like. The poles are really very long cylinders. If you look up at a cylinder, you see something like this ➔

If you look down at a cylinder, you see something like this*

When you stand near a power pole, you look *up* at the top and *down* at the bottom, so the *top* curves *up* and the *bottom* curves *down.* Your eye level (the horizon) is somewhere in between. You can change the eye level in a new drawing by placing the horizon higher or lower on your page. Usually it's somewhere in the middle.

Low horizon—low eye level

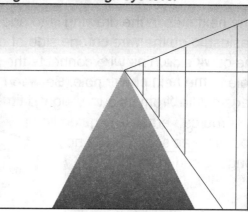

High Horizon—high eye level

* *Learn To Draw NOW!* introduces cylinders and other essential 3-D forms.

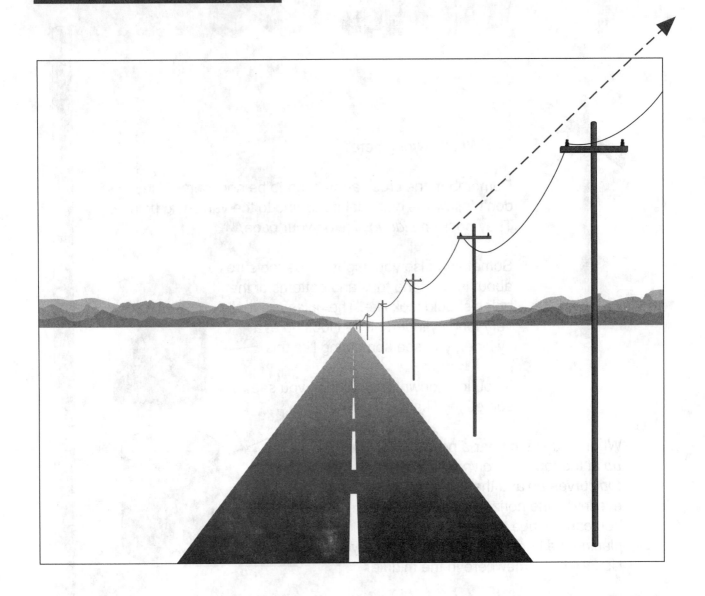

The next step in the drawing is to add wires to the poles. You'll find it easiest to do the wire on one side of each pole first, then the wire on the other side. The wire connects the same point on each power pole to the next power pole. Between poles, the wire sags a little (from its own weight).

You can erase any guide lines you draw as soon as you no longer need them.

▼ **IMPORTANT!**
Note that the guide lines have disappeared from my picture. (You did draw them very lightly, didn't you?)

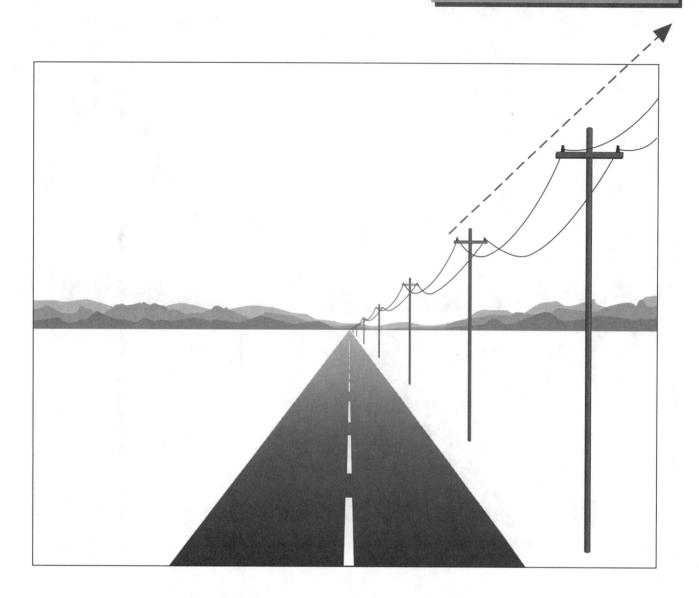

The second wire does exactly the same thing—it connects at the same point on each pole, and sags a little in between. Notice how the wires continue out of the picture at the top right, in the same direction.

Let's add some clouds to make the picture more interesting.

If you made mistakes on your first drawing, don't worry! But if your paper has gotten really messy, you might want to start over with another piece before making the drawing more complicated. When you're ready to continue, the next step is to add another light guide line to the left of the road, where the shadows of the power poles will fall.

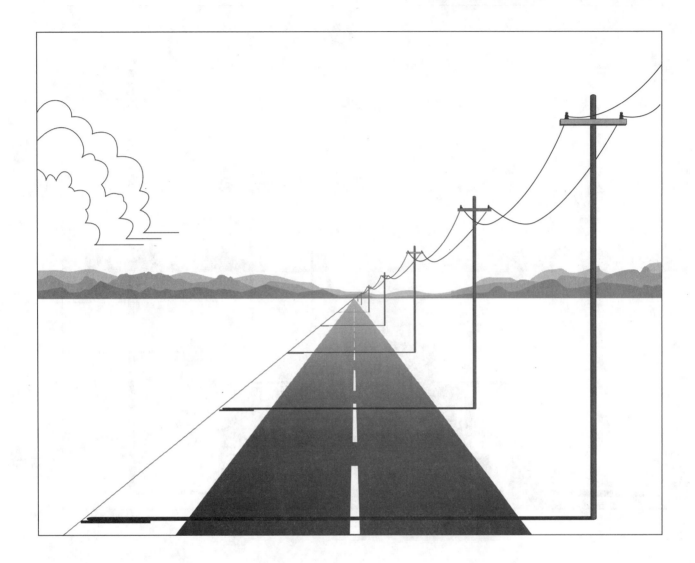

To keep things simple, I'm pretending the sun is shining from overhead, off the right side of the picture. Looking down this road, you would feel the sun on your right shoulder, and the right side of your face.

The shadows of the power poles would fall to the left, horizontally, starting from the very bottom of each pole and extending to the guide line. Draw the shadow of each pole. (By the way, you would hardly see *any* shadow of the cross arms if the sun was directly to the side.)

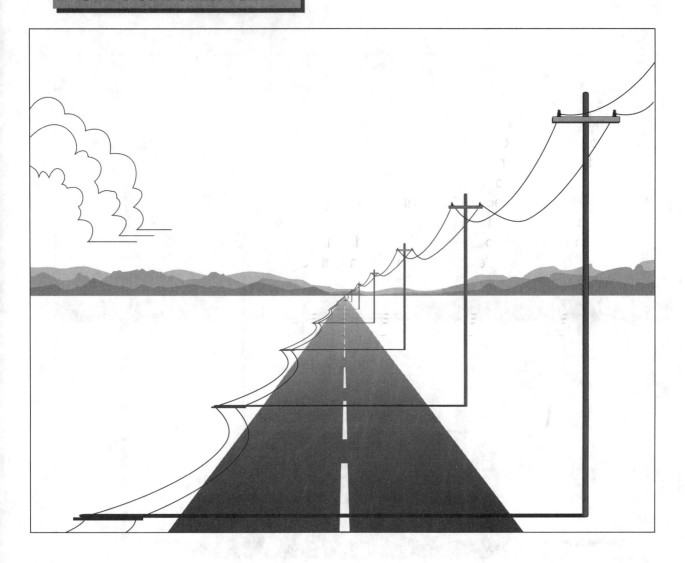

You'd also see shadows of the wires. Add them to your picture. Can you see how each detail that you add creates more depth in the picture? It's important, of course, that each of the details follows the basic rules.

TIME OUT!

Let's review some of the key points we've covered so far:

1. Objects farther away are smaller. They're usually closer to the vanishing point;

2. Horizontal lines going *away from you* get closer together (example: the sides of the road). In one-point perspective, everything going *away* from you heads towards a vanishing point;

3. In one-point perspective, verticals go straight up and down. Horizontals follow the horizon, from side to side.

One other very important point: your drawing doesn't have to look like mine, or anyone else's: the idea is to have fun. Invent your own landscape! I'll give you some more ideas in a few pages....

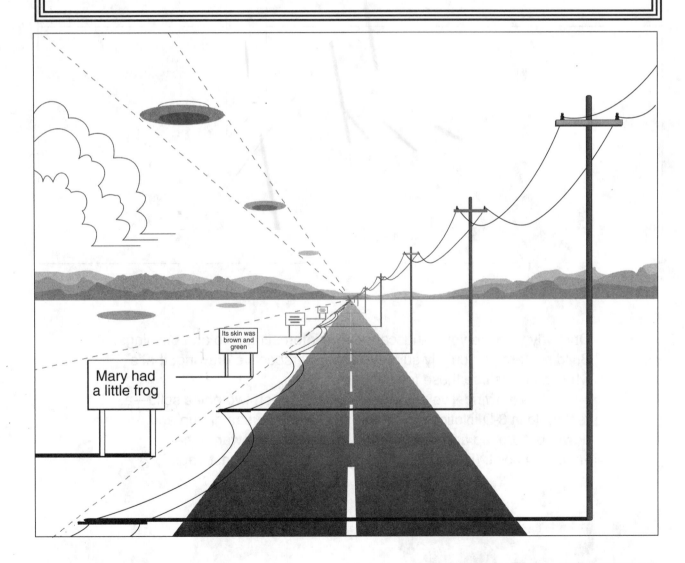

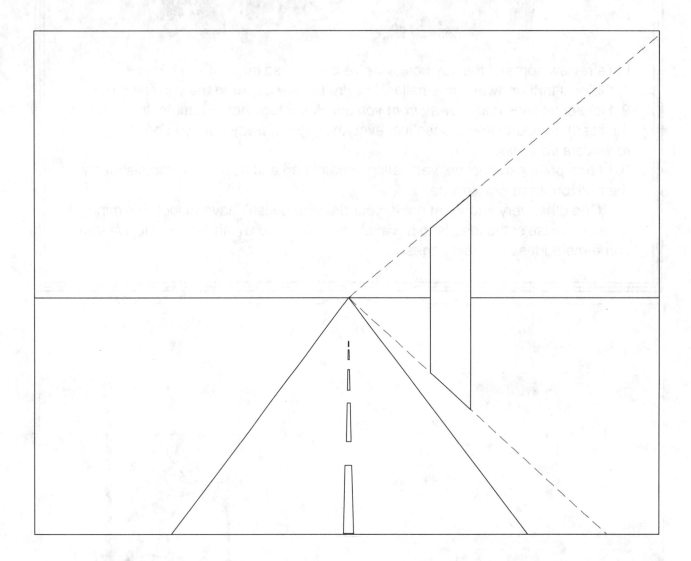

One way to make your landscape more interesting is to add buildings. Buildings are particularly suited to linear perspective drawing; that's why architects use these techniques so often.

In this drawing, I've made the space between two poles solid—a rectangle in 3-D. Notice how the vertical sides go straight up and down, but the top and bottom of the rectangle go towards the vanishing point. (Remember the key points from the last page?)

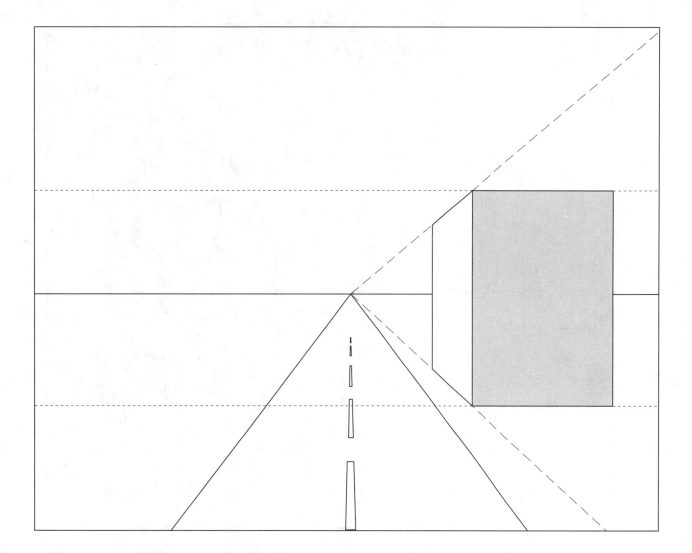

To make the rectangle into a box (like a building), draw horizontal lines running from side to side for the top and bottom (same as the crossarms on the power poles), then add another vertical to complete the rectangle.

I'm adding shading to help you see the different pieces of the puzzle. If you want to add shading to your drawing, the best thing is to wait until you have all of the shapes drawn, then shade them all at once, making sure that you know where the light is coming from.

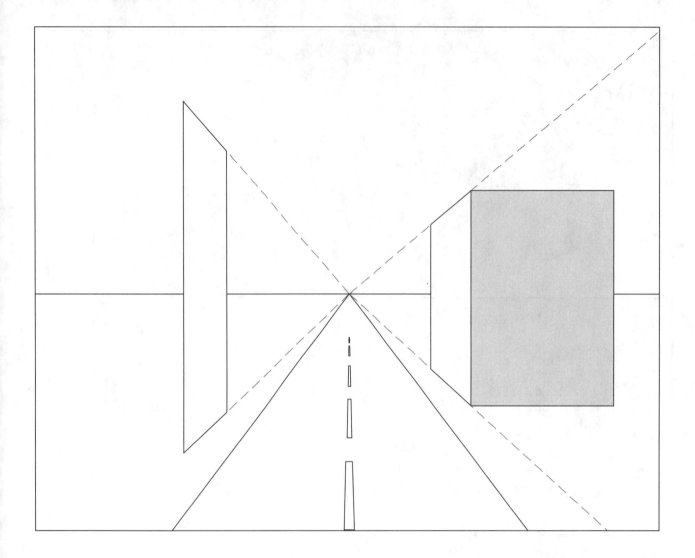

You can make as many buildings as you can fit in the picture. Add the guide lines very lightly.

No matter how many times you draw this type of picture, it's still very difficult to make everything look right without guidelines… especially details like doors and windows, which we'll get to next. Be patient—and always start out drawing very lightly!

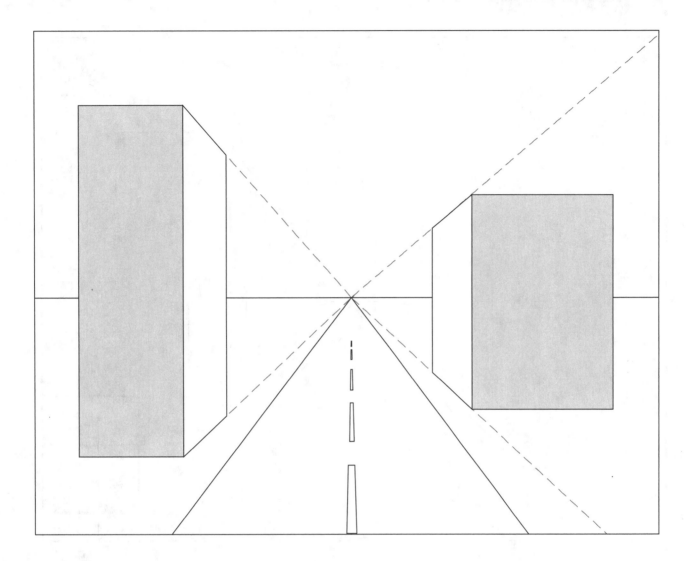

On this new building, I've added the side facing you—the side that has just horizontal and vertical lines. Remember, only the lines going *away* from you converge on the vanishing point.

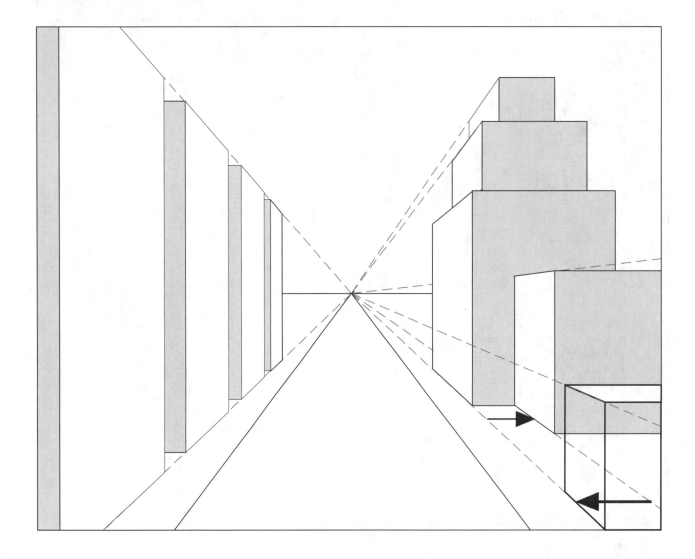

Add as many buildings as you like. Your buildings don't all have to be in a straight line. Here, the buildings on the left side of the road line up with one guide line—perhaps a sidewalk. But the buildings on the right side of the road line up on a couple of different guide lines, making it look as though one of the buildings is set back from the street.

If this drawing seems complicated, that's probably because it has several layers, front to back. But they all follow the same rules!

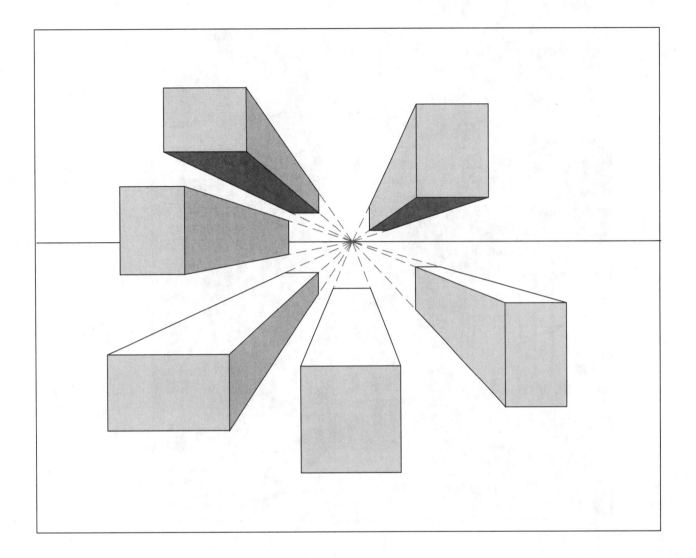

Remember the first drawings we did, of shapes extending towards the vanishing point? Here's a new effect to try with those drawings: instead of extending the lines *all the way* to the vanishing point, cut them short, and add back edges to the shape. As you experiment, you'll discover that it's quite easy to make some shapes look closer, and some farther away.

You might also think about looking *down* into the drawing... With a little imagination, you can place yourself high above a city square, looking down....

Can you see how this drawing resembles the drawing on the previous page? Can you figure out where the vanishing point is?

Vanishing point

The same technique works
when you're looking up!

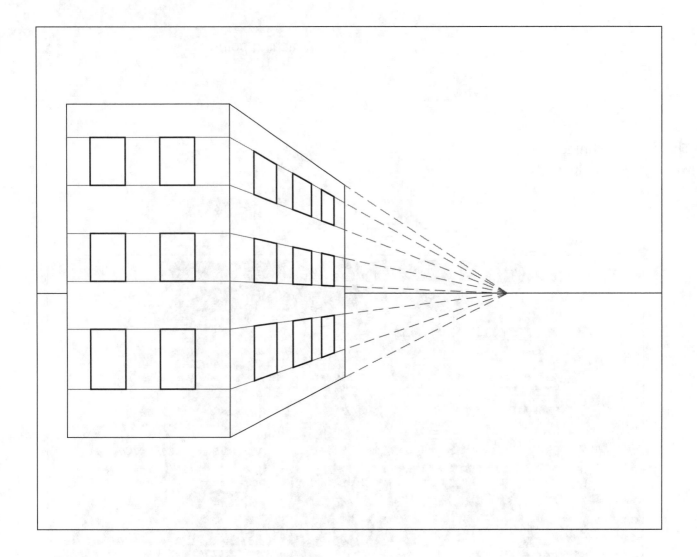

To make linear perspective work, you always need to pay attention to how your lines create the effect you want. The lines which converge on the vanishing point (or point towards it) create the sense of depth in the picture.

Other lines reinforce the sense of depth. In the buildings, these are the lines running across the paper—lines which *don't* point towards the vanishing point. Try to use both types of lines carefully when you draw in perspective, and watch to see when they help, and when they don't….

Above, you see an example of the lines directing your eye towards the vanishing point. Below, notice the lines running up and down, and back and forth—reinforcing the feeling of depth. It will take some practice to develop a feel for the spacing of this second type of line, but keep working on it. The effect is worth it!

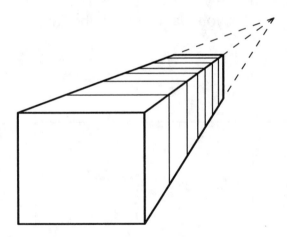

Notice! Part of the building on the preceding page is above the horizon, and part of it is below the horizon. In a landscape picture, that means part of the building is above eye level and part of it is below eye level. The two drawings on this page are below eye level: you're looking down on them.

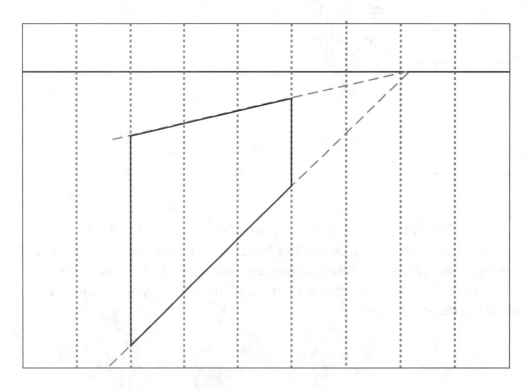

Let's look at those lines step by step, and make sure you understand which are which. First, there are the lines running towards the vanishing point (above).

Next, there are the lines running up and down—vertical on the paper (when you make the vertical lines, look at the edges of your paper, not at the lines you've already drawn).

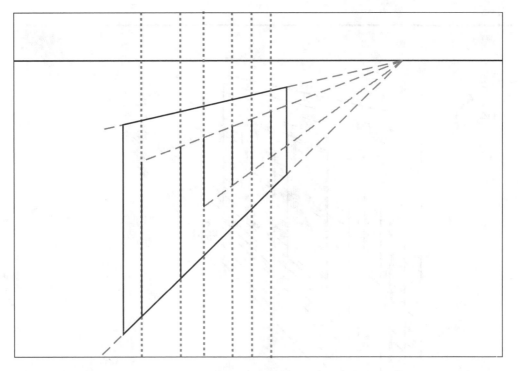

Any vertical lines on this wall go straight up and down. Draw evenly spaced objects, such as windows, closer together as they get farther away. It will take some practice to get the spacing right. Your first few tries probably won't look perfect...so what?

Finally, you can finish the tops and bottoms of doors and windows using additional guide lines running towards the vanishing point.

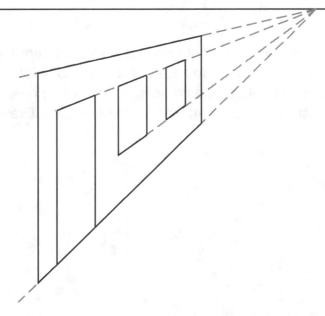

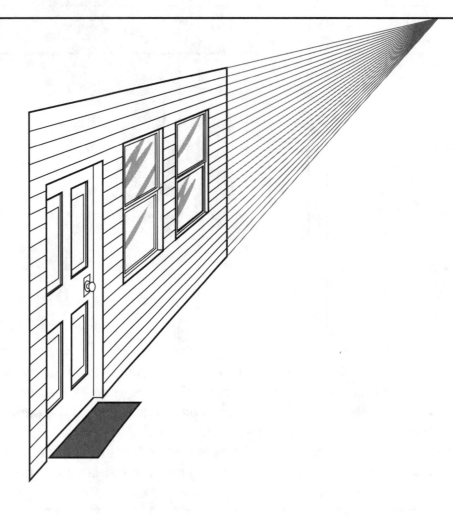

Adding more details can enhance the feeling of depth. But the more details you add, the more careful you have to be about following the rules. Even a couple of lines running in the wrong direction can ruin the whole effect. Use your ruler. Remember the rules. Draw *carefully!*

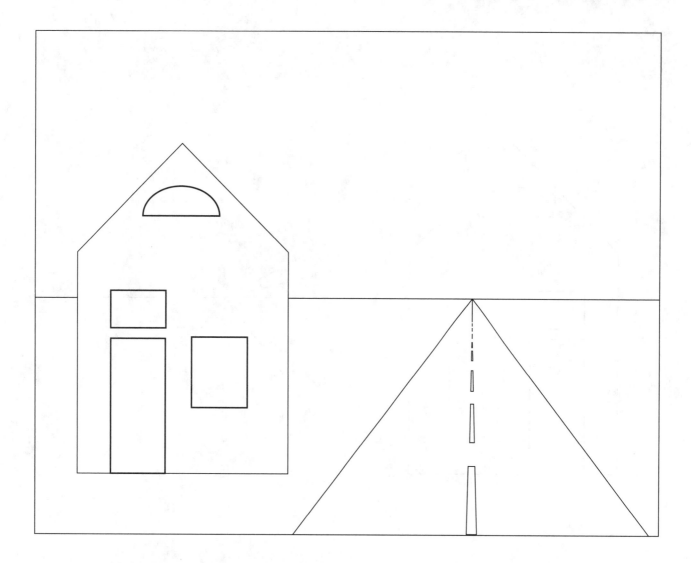

Now that we've looked at complicated examples of three-dimensional drawing, let's get back to basics. Remember that house you used to draw and paint when you were in kindergarten? Let's see if we can put it in three dimensions.

Go ahead—draw it (just the front—no chimney!).

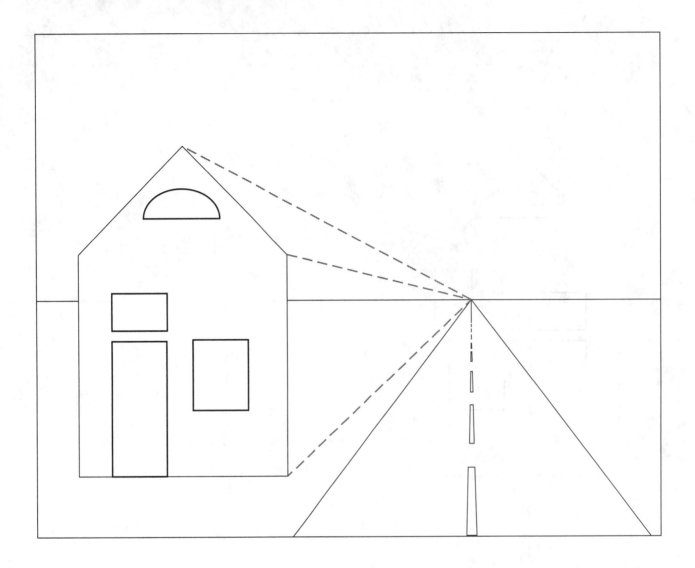

Now extend the sides back towards the vanishing point (yes, I know this doesn't seem right, but think of the earlier drawings in this book). As you first draw the lines, remember that they're just guide lines—keep them light enough to erase later!

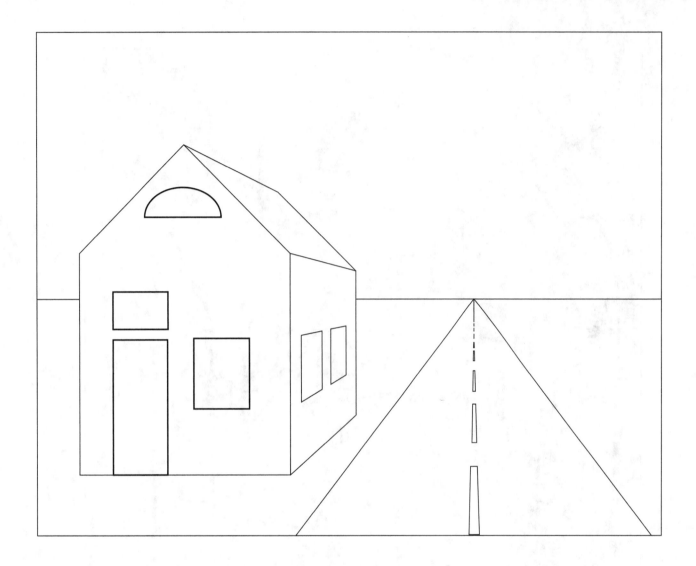

Now, 'chop off' the back of the house with a vertical line and a line parallel to the roof line. Add details on the side if you want. If you have trouble, go back and follow the steps, one at a time.

If you've never tried this kind of drawing before, don't be surprised if it seems odd—or if your first efforts look strange. As with all new things that you learn, it may take a while before this kind of drawing makes sense. It's like learning a new language. Just keep at it, and all of a sudden you'll start to understand it...!

So far, most of the drawings in this book have been very tight and neat. That's to show you how perspective works. When you start a real drawing, you'll probably want to sketch your ideas first, without worrying if the perspective is perfect.

Later, when you've decided exactly what you want your drawing to look like, you can clean up lines that aren't right. Or, as I did in this drawing, you may want to start over with a clean sheet of paper.

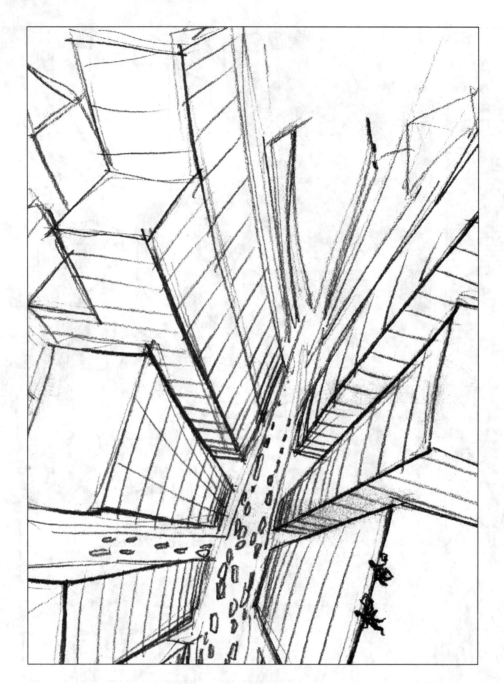

In this sketch, notice that the street runs at an angle, instead of being perfectly vertical. Also, the lines curve slightly, imitating a camera's wide-angle lens. Both help create an unsettling effect in the picture.

Here are other examples of scenes I invented,
imagining I was high in the air looking down. In each,
look at how the converging lines follow the rules of
one-point perspective.

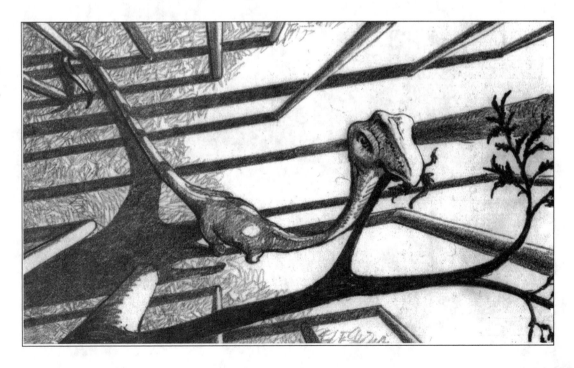

Examples of perspective are all around you. Look at buildings and bridges, and notice how the lines converge. Not all examples are straight lines. In the drawing below, you can see that perspective applies to curved lines, as well. They also converge on a single vanishing point.

CHAPTER 3
TWO-POINT PERSPECTIVE

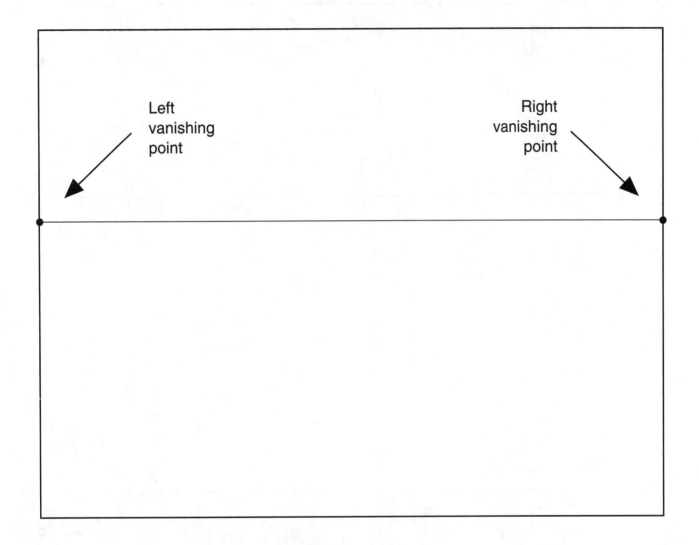

Left
vanishing
point

Right
vanishing
point

What we're going to do next—a drawing in two-point perspective—may seem confusing at first. Do each step carefully, and try to make your drawing just like the one in the book. That way, if you lose track of which lines go where, you can back up a step or two.

Once you master the basics, please don't follow the book—because when you use your imagination, that's when the real fun begins! Make up your own buildings, and try more complex drawings using these techniques.

Our two-point perspective drawing starts out with a horizon, and a vanishing point at either end. Remember, each vanishing point needs only be big enough, and dark enough, so that you can see it.

Next, below the horizon, make a small vertical line. Notice that mine isn't exactly in the middle. It's off a little bit to the left.

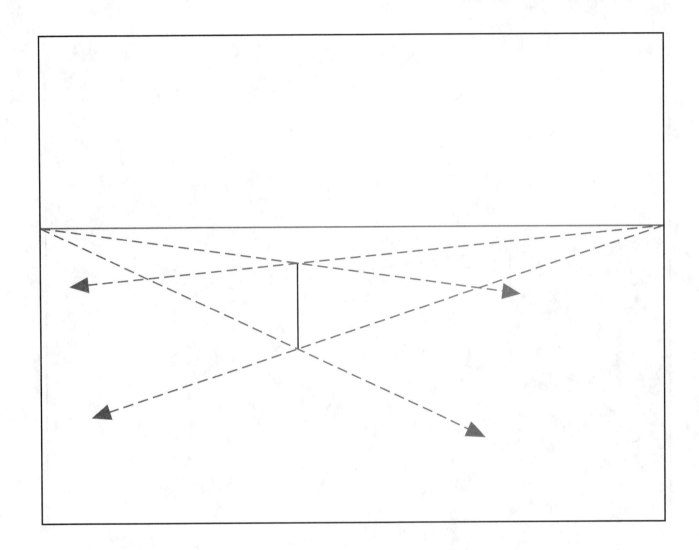

From each vanishing point, draw two lines, one touching the top, and one touching the bottom of your small vertical line. Notice how the new lines look like they're zooming toward you. The lines go *down* the page from the vanishing points. (They are *below* eye level; lines going *up* from the vanishing point would be *above* eye level.)

▼ **IMPORTANT!**
Remember to make lines very light at first! Not all of them will be part of the finished picture!

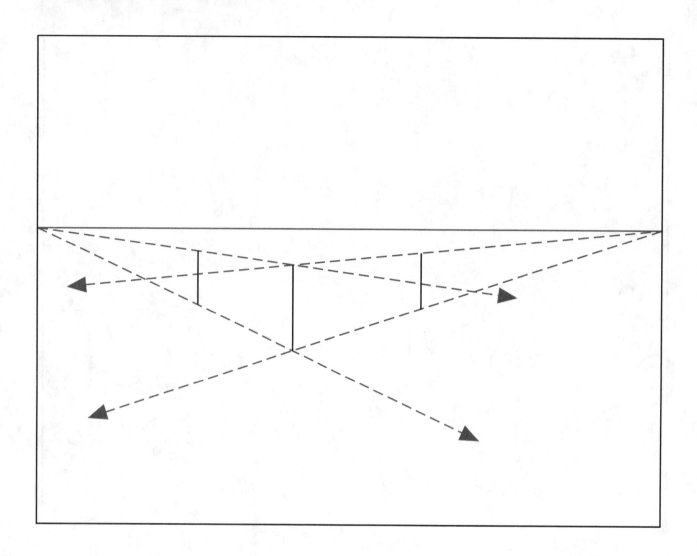

Next add two more vertical lines. Can you figure out what we're
drawing? These lines show where the far corners of the house will be.

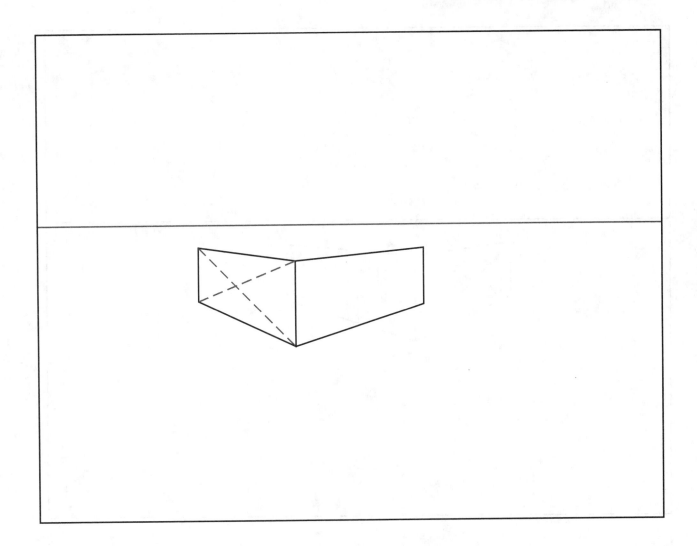

The roof comes next—but first we need to find the center of the wall, so that we know where to put the peak of the roof. To find the center of the wall, draw diagonals: make an "X" that connects the corners. The center of the "X" shows the center of the wall—in perspective.

To see why we have to go to such trouble to find the center of the wall, try locating the center of the wall by measuring with your ruler. When you measure with a ruler, you can find the center of the line, but not the center of the shape in 3-D.

To create a 3-D drawing, you always have to follow the rules....

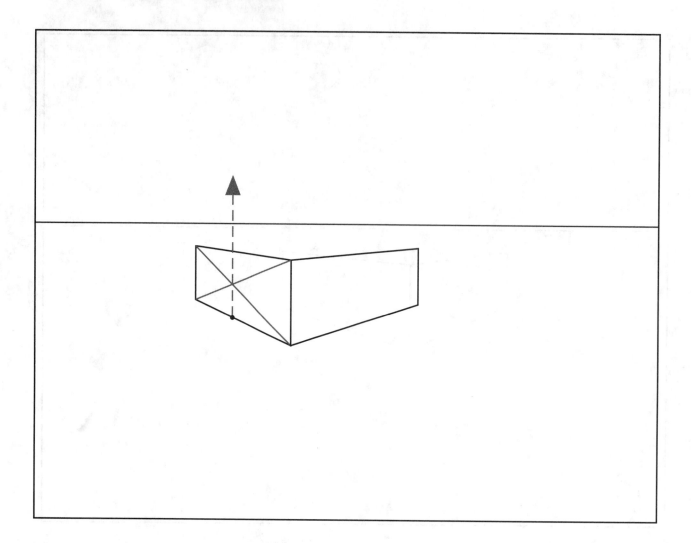

From the middle of the wall—the crossing point of the "X"—make a vertical line (straight up). Wherever you stop, that will be the peak of the roof. I've made mine above the horizon. You could stop below the horizon, or even right on the horizon—but if the top of the roof is exactly even with the horizon, it will be confusing. For your first picture, follow my example, and make the roof above the horizon.

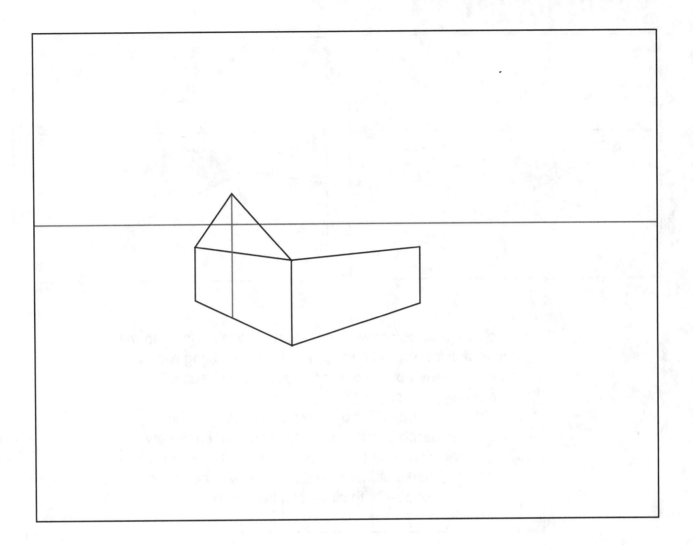

Think of the vertical line as a post that holds up the peak of the roof. Connect the corners of the house to it with lines (they would be rafters in a real house).

Note: this is a 'wide-angle' drawing. After a few more pages, I'll tell you more about locating the vanishing points to make the drawing look more 'normal.' As you practice, you can refine your technique.

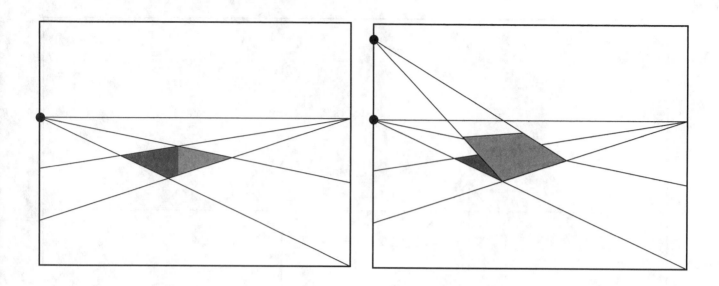

Here's a quick look at what comes next. We're going to make the roof slant. An inclined plane (like the slanting roof) is not parallel to the bottom of the house, and it needs different vanishing points.

Imagine a trap door opening. Because of its hinge, it stays parallel as it opens. As it moves, each new vanishing point is directly above or below the others. (When it points straight up, it's like the wall of the house—both sides can be drawn parallel.)

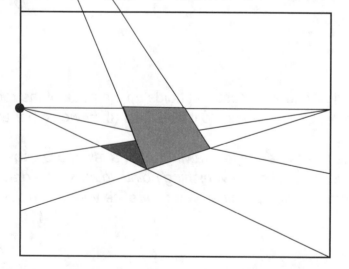

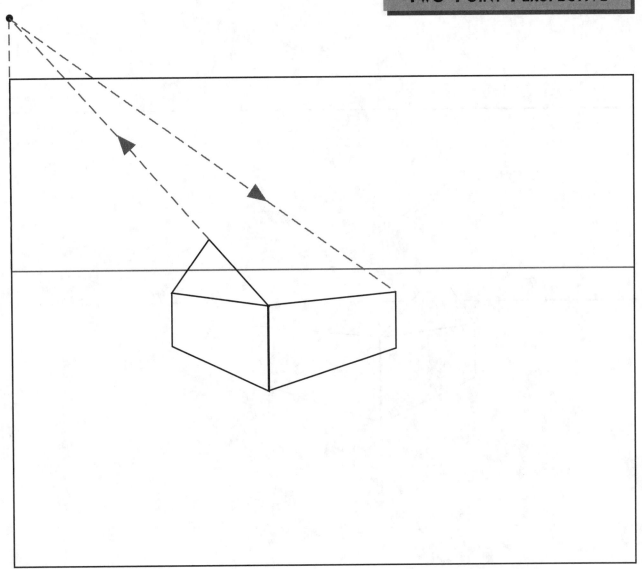

Now you can see the 'proper' way to draw the roof. The front of the roof extends to a point directly above the left vanishing point, making the roof vanishing point. From the roof vanishing point, a line extends back to the far corner of the house, making the back end of the roof.

Less 'proper,' but much easier: just draw it. After a couple of tries, it will probably look fine, without fussing with all the lines!

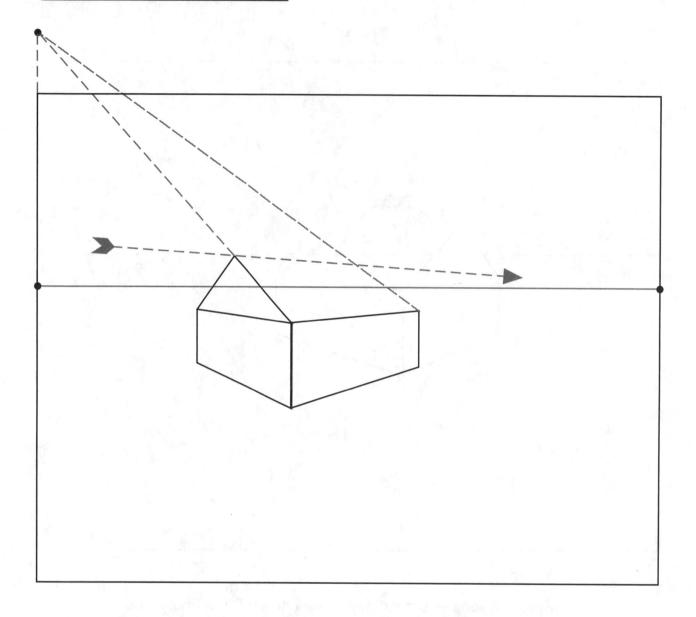

Next, draw a line from the peak of the roof towards the right vanishing point. Now you see the entire top of the roof, from front to back. You don't need to draw the line all the way to the vanishing point—just far enough to find the peak of the back slope of the roof.

Important: the top of the roof is NOT parallel to the horizon!

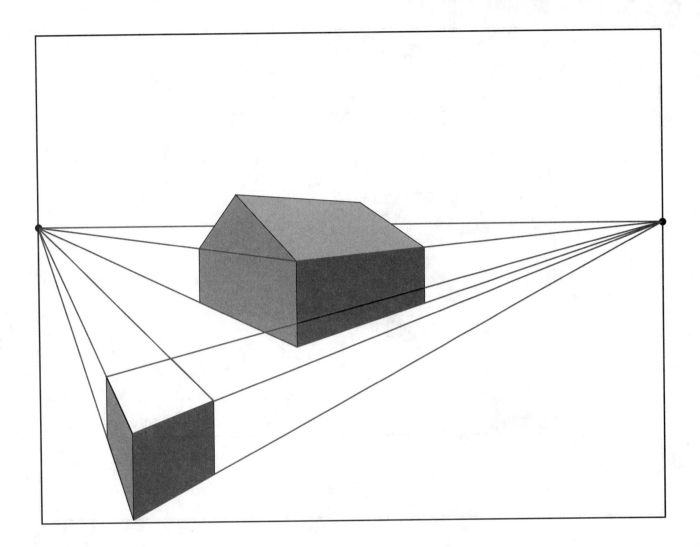

This is a "wide-angle" drawing, because it's similar to looking through a wide-angle lens on a camera. Where you can run into problems with this drawing is when you place objects too close to the edge of the frame, as I have done with the box in the lower left.

The problem is not with the frame of the picture—although you can use the frame to fix it, as you'll see on the next page. The problem is that the vanishing points are too close together. This creates a distorted view. At the end of the book, you'll find photos of buildings, and you'll see that the vanishing points are well outside of the picture frame. That's the usual way perspective drawings are done.

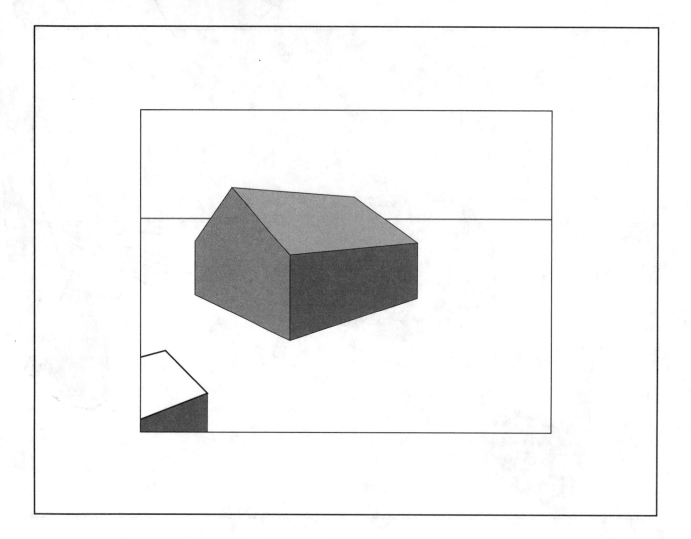

When you make the frame of the picture smaller (in this case, cutting off part of the box) the drawing starts to look more normal. With the frame smaller, the vanishing points are outside the picture.

For most two-point perspective drawing, the vanishing points are well outside the picture frame. It's more complicated to draw that way: you have to fasten the paper down to the drawing surface, get a longer ruler, and so forth. But it's a view that people are used to: once again, refer to the photos of buildings in the back of the book.

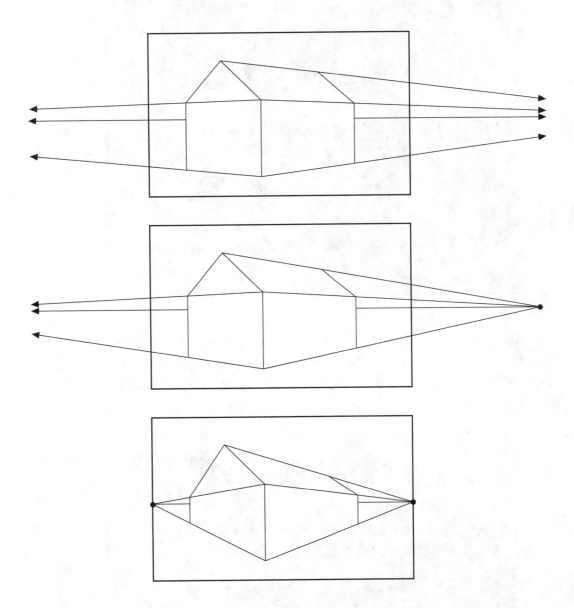

These diagrams show how the drawing changes as the vanishing points are moved. In the top drawing, the vanishing points are so far to either side that you don't see them on the page. This is equivalent to looking through a telephoto lens on a camera.

The middle drawing is a more "normal" view. The bottom drawing, with the vanishing points at the edge of the picture frame, is very distorted.

What's the difference between these two pictures?

Look at the lines of the front and side of the truck—can you start to see where you would place the vanishing points if you were drawing?

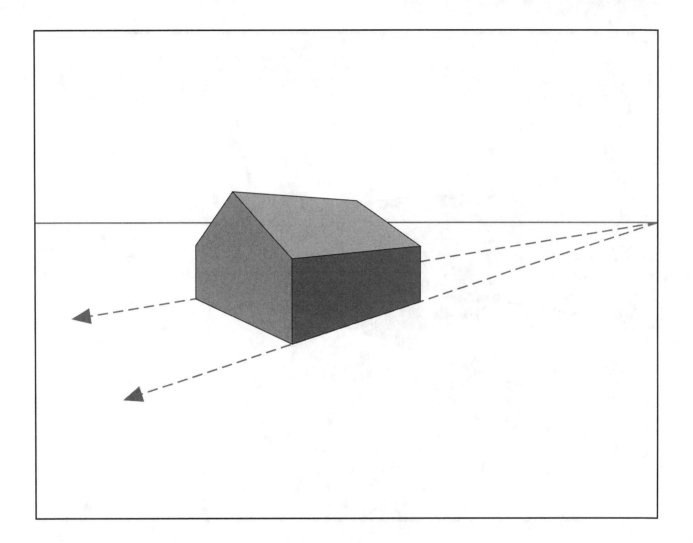

There's still room on our house drawing. Let's build an addition!
    Extend two walls of the house from the right vanishing point. (To build an addition on a real house, you would lay out lines with string tied to little wooden posts, very similar to this drawing.)

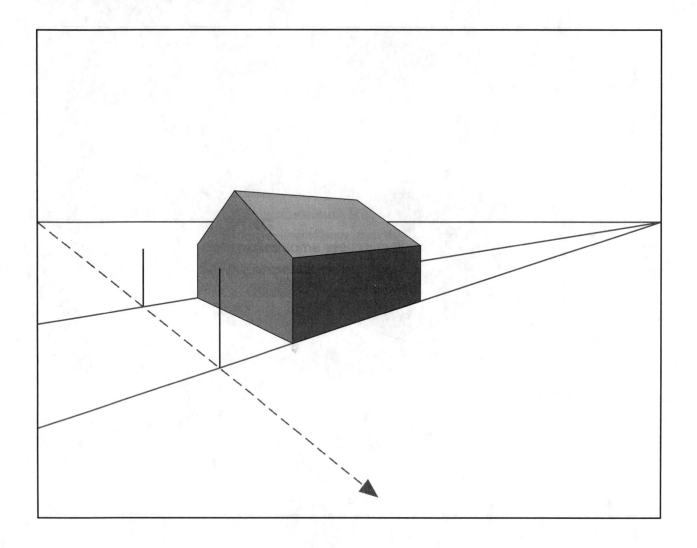

Next, draw a line from the left vanishing point to mark the bottom of the wall. This wall will be parallel to the wall of the house, because it uses the same vanishing point.

Where the line crosses the first two lines (from the right vanishing point), add vertical lines.

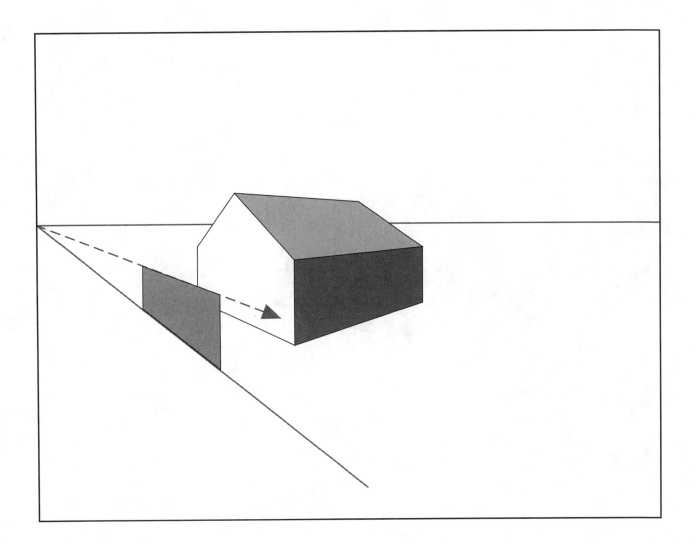

With another line from the left vanishing point, you can mark the top of the wall . You don't have to draw the line beyond where you actually need it, but in the beginning, you'll find it helpful to draw (lightly!) all the way to the vanishing point. As with the other guide lines, erase them when they're no longer needed.

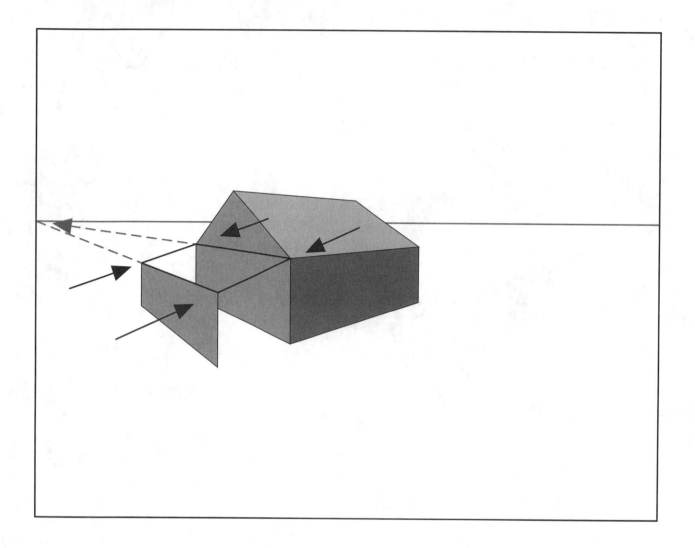

Now connect the corners of the new wall with the existing wall of the house. The line where the roof connects to the house should point towards the left vanishing point.

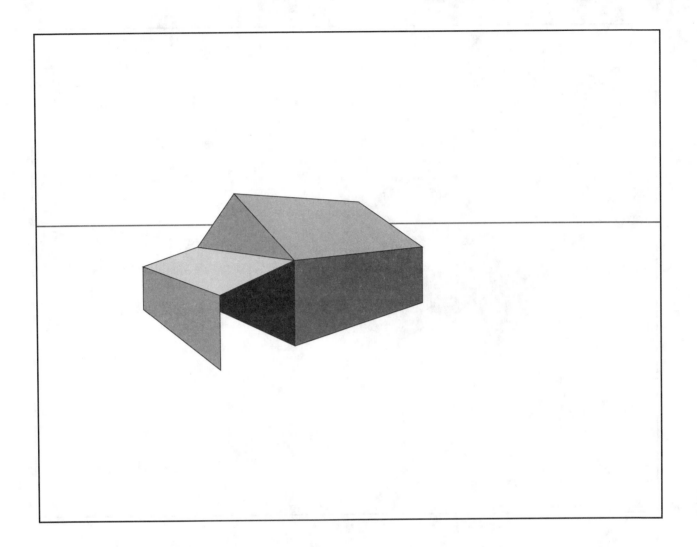

So here we have it—a handy shed or carport, in which to store firewood, broken toys and bicycles, old washing machines, worn out tires, and all kinds of other great stuff!

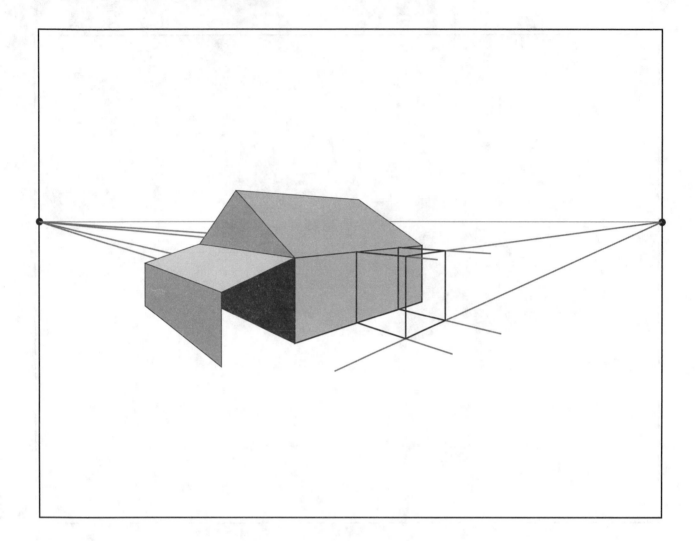

Now—how about a breakfast nook?

I'll go faster this time. Here I've drawn a box as an addition. Notice that I've been careful to use the correct vanishing point for each wall. (And the vertical lines go straight up and down!) I probably wouldn't actually draw the lines to the left of the house, but I would watch carefully while drawing, to make sure my ruler stayed lined up on the vanishing point—it's easy for the ruler to slip just a tiny bit, which can make the drawing look strange.

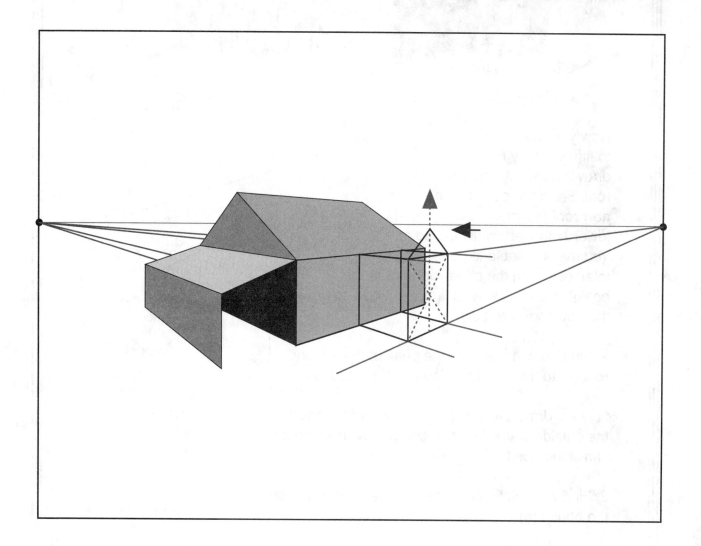

As with the peak of the first roof, I'm using an "X" to find the center of
the wall, and extending it upwards to the peak. You can decide how
high you want this one to be.

TIME OUT!

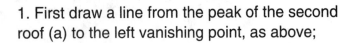

Now you have
to figure a way to
draw the rest of the
roof. From the peak of the
new roof (a), make a line
towards the left vanishing point.
You might be able to guess where it
intersects with the other roof (not at the
peak!). Here's a way to figure out how to draw
the new roof precisely:

1. First draw a line from the peak of the second
roof (a) to the left vanishing point, as above;

2. Next, draw a line from the middle of the top of
the outside wall of the addition (b) towards the left
vanishing point;

3. Find the point where that line meets the wall of
the house (c);

4. From point (c), draw a line towards
the roof vanishing point. Where it
crosses the first line
(Step 1) marks the point
where the two roofs meet.
Connect that with the
corner where the walls meet
and you're all done! (Except,
of course, for erasing all those
extra guide lines going all over
the place!)

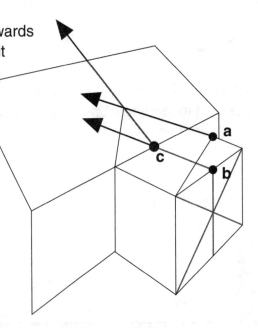

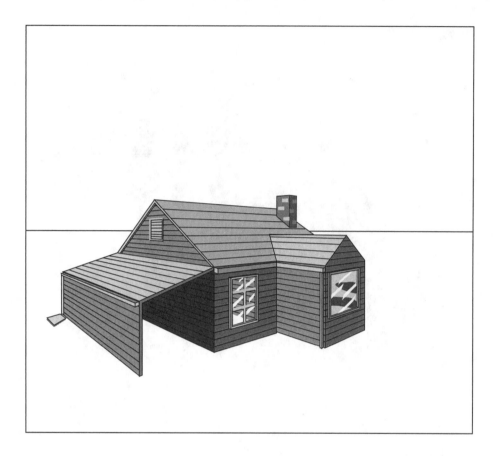

If you managed to get that second addition built on the house (or even if you didn't), you'll probably want to add some details like doors and windows, gutters, and perhaps a chimney. Take care to line up anything horizontal on the building with one of the two vanishing points, and remember that vertical lines are always vertical in this drawing.

The next step is to add shadows, because shadows help create depth. Shadows in your drawing don't have to be perfect—they just have to look good! In the next few pages, we'll see how to draw shadows for this house, using the rules.

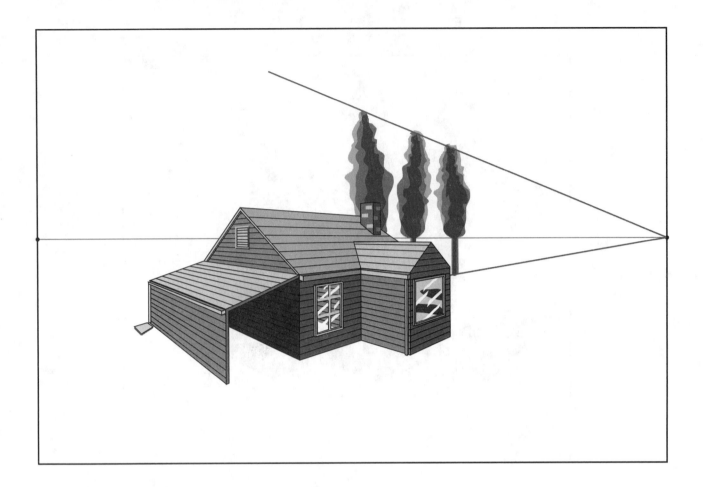

Before we tackle the house shadows (which are complicated), let's try some simple shadows. Where we live, you often see rows of poplar trees. They're tall, thin trees that people plant close together in neat lines to form windbreaks. The idea is to keep the cold winter wind from blasting directly on your house or fields. Usually, poplars are planted in straight lines along roads, or at the edges of fields.

In this drawing, I'm adding three poplar trees, lined up with the house and the right vanishing point. They were planted at the same time, so they're the same height—meaning that one line connects the tops to the vanishing point. They're in a straight line parallel to the house, so the bottoms also make one line to the horizon.

Of course, to have shadows, you need a light source, so I've added the sun. Notice that it's *outside* the drawing! It's fairly easy to figure out that a line from the sun, touching the top of a tree, would show you where the shadow falls. But to find the place where it stops, you need to go one step further, and find the shadow vanishing point.

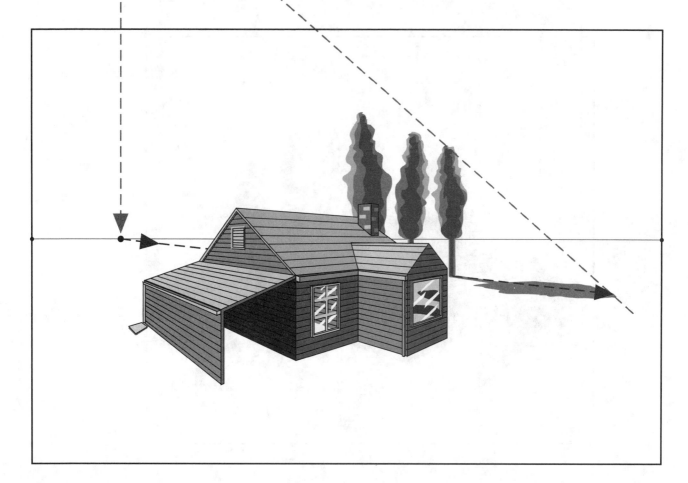

To find the shadow vanishing point, locate a point on the horizon directly beneath the sun (or other light source). A line from the shadow vanishing point, through the point on the ground directly below the top of the tree, intersects the ray from the sun exactly where the shadow should stop.

You can probably draw the shadow perfectly well without plotting everything out, but it's helpful to know the rules!

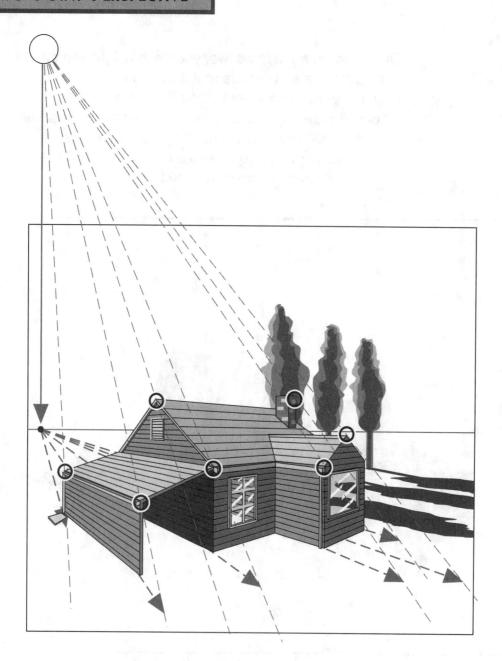

Here's how the same principle works with the high points of the house. The circles show points on the house that may appear in the shadow on the ground—corners, peaks, and edges. As before, a line from the shadow vanishing point, through the point on the ground directly below circled point on the house, intersects the ray from the sun exactly where the shadow should stop.

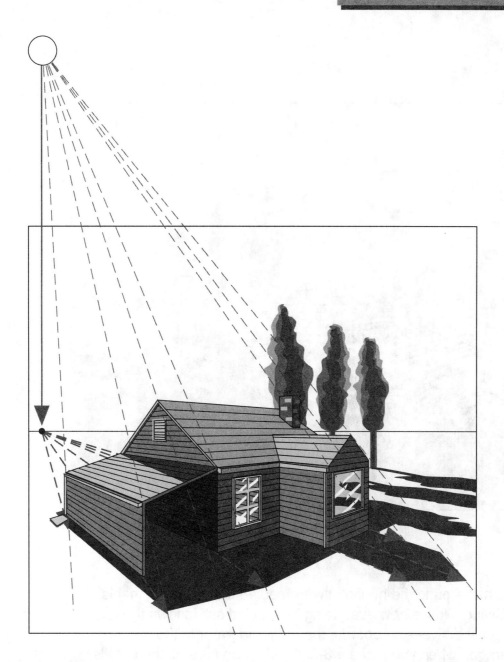

    Not all of the points may show up when the shadow is complete. Adding the shadow then becomes a game of connect-the-dots. If you already have a pretty good idea what the shadow should look like, you might try drawing them without all this fuss. You can always use this technique when you want to be more precise. But most pictures won't need to be entirely precise, since few people really study the shadows!

    At this point, get rid of those guide lines. Take a deep breath and look at your picture. How does it look? Do you sense there's something still missing? Something like…

...**stuff** around the house? I've remedied that situation in this drawing. Notice how everything I've added still follows the rules of perspective—the boards, the old refrigerator in the garage...when you make a 3-D drawing, be sure all the details work together to create the illusion of depth.

Here's an example of vanishing point lines in an actual photo. I haven't taken them all the way to the vanishing points because, as you can see, the vanishing points would be well off the paper! Because this is so often the case, you won't always want to actually plot vanishing points—but once you've done it a few times, you'll start to see the angles. As you keep practicing, it will seem more normal, and become easier to draw.

As you practice perspective drawing, you'll find it helpful to use photos—perhaps from a book or magazine. Try drawing this house—and try it *without* tracing. Tracing is a useful way to transfer the basics of an image, but right now your eye needs practice—so draw this by looking at it only. Want some hints?

1) First locate the horizon—near the floor of the front porch.
2) Draw your verticals—very lightly, of course!
3) Locate approximate vanishing points.
4) Actually lay your pencil or ruler on top of the photo, vertically or horizontally, to compare angles as you draw.

I've chosen this Victorian house because it has such great details. When you draw a house like this, those details attract the viewer's attention—this means the viewer probably won't notice (or be bothered) if your perspective is a little off. Even if your perspective is off by a lot, don't give up! Add lots of detail, and carefully color the house as brightly as possible. No one but you will even notice the perspective!

Remember what I said about using your imagination? How about inventing your own landscape—go wild! Have fun! Use your imagination! Now that you know some of the techniques for creating 3-D drawings, it's up to you to figure out new ways to use them.

REMEMBER...

1. Practice

One of the great secrets of our world is that behind every success there's always plenty of practice. The people who do amazing feats of daring, skill, or ingenuity have been practicing, often for much longer than you'd imagine. They've probably failed more often than you can imagine, too, so don't waste time being discouraged. If your drawings don't look exactly the way you'd like them to, especially when you start out with a new idea, figure out what went wrong, and do it again right!

2. Save your drawings!

Whenever you do a drawing—or even a sketch—put your initials (or autograph!) and date on it. And save it. You don't have to save it until it turns yellow and crumbles to dust, but do keep your drawings, at least for several months. Sometimes, hiding in your portfolio, they will mysteriously improve—! I've seen it happen often with my own drawings, especially the ones I knew were no good at all, but kept anyway....

To keep your drawings neat, make a *portfolio* of your own. (You can also buy a ready-made one at an art supply store.)

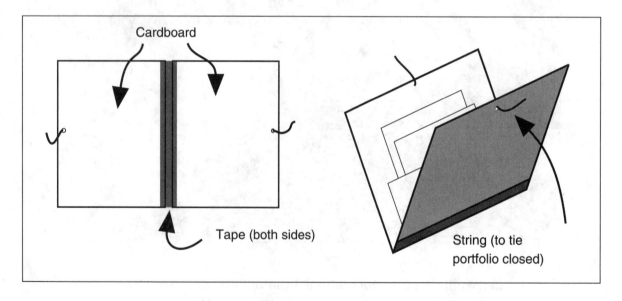

Cardboard

Tape (both sides)

String (to tie portfolio closed)